SCIENCE CORNER

Forces: Pushes and Pulls

Angela Royston

PowerKiDS press.

New York

Published in 2012 by The Rosen Publishing Group Inc.
29 East 21st Street, New York, NY 10010

First Edition

Editor: Katie Powell
Designer: Robert Walster
Picture Researcher: Diana Morris

Library of Congress Cataloging-in-Publication Data

Royston, Angela, 1945-
Forces : Pushes and Pulls / By Angela Royston. — 1st. ed.
        pages cm. — (Science Corner)
Includes index.
ISBN 978-1-4488-5292-5 (library binding)
1. Force and energy—Juvenile literature. 2. Motion—Juvenile
literature. I. Title.
QC73.4.R693 2012
531'.6—dc22

                              2010046293

Photographs:
Don Bayley/istockphoto: 17. John Bloor/istockphoto: 2, 8.
Bronwyn photo/istockphoto: 16. Christian Carrol/istockphoto:
10. Rob Friedman/istockphoto: 15. Juice Images/Alamy: 6.
Herbert Kim/istockphoto: 21. Paul Kline/istockphoto: 14.
Josef Muellek/istockphoto: 1, 18. Catalin Petolea/
Shutterstock: 7. Pixland/Corbis: 11. Eve Serrabassa/
istockphoto: 19. Steve Shepard/istockphoto: 4. Jacoms
Stephens/istockphoto: 9. Steve Stone/istockphoto: 12.
Leah-Anne Thompson/istockphoto: front cover, 13.
Valenty/istockphoto: 20. Wayland: 22, 23.
Artmann Witt/istockphoto: 5.

Manufactured in China
CPSIA Compliance Information: Batch #WAS1102PK: For Further Information
contact Rosen Publishing, New York, New York at 1-800-237-9932

Web Sites

Due to the changing nature of Internet
links, PowerKids Press has developed
an online list of Web sites related to
the subject of this book. This site is
updated regularly. Please use this link
to access this list:
http://www.powerkidslinks.com/sc/forces/

Contents

Pushing and Pulling

Pushing and pulling are both forces.
Some forces are small. It only takes
a small force to push a toy truck.

Other forces are big. It takes a big force to push a heavy car.

 # Pushes

A push sends something away from you.

You push a supermarket cart to make it move.

Sometimes you push with your hands and arms. But you have to push with your foot when you ride a scooter.

When you kick a ball, you push it with your foot.

 # Pulls

A pull brings something toward you.

For example, you pull open a drawer.

Wheels make it easier to pull
all kinds of things. Most suitcases
have wheels to make them
easy to pull.

How Things Move

When you are on a swing, you move forward and backward. A seesaw moves up and down.

Other things move in a circle. You turn
the pedals of a bicycle to make the
wheels go around.

A merry-go-round moves around in a circle.

Making Things Move Faster

A force can make something move faster. The harder you push the pedals of a bike, the faster the bike moves.

The harder you push a toy car,
the faster it moves. When you stop
pushing, the car slows down.

Changing Direction

Pushing and pulling can make something change direction. This dog is on a leash. The owner pulls the leash to make the dog change direction.

When you hit a ball with a bat, the ball changes direction. The ball stops coming toward you and spins away from you instead.

Slowing Things Down

A force can slow down or stop something that is moving. When you catch a ball, you stop it moving.

Warning!
Don't try to stop something heavy. It could knock you down.

Bicycles, cars, and other vehicles all have brakes to make them slow down. A brake pushes a block against the wheel to slow the wheel down.

wheel

brake block

Force of the Wind

Wind is moving air. The faster the air moves, the stronger the wind. When you fly a kite, the force of the wind lifts the kite into the air.

Wind is a natural force, because it is not made by people. People can use natural forces to work machines.

The force of the wind turns the blades of a wind turbine to make electricity.

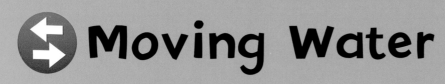 # Moving Water

Moving water is also a natural force. Water runs downhill into streams and rivers.

The water can push along leaves, twigs, and logs.

Waves are moving water. Big waves hit the shore with a huge force.

Car Chase

Try this simple experiment to discover more about the force of pushing.

You will need:
- a toy car
- a piece of black paper
- a measuring tape
- some chalk

1. Mark a cross on a piece of black paper with the chalk.

2. Put the car on the cross and push it as hard as you can with your finger.

3. Measure how
far the car goes.

4. Ask your friend to
take a turn. Make sure
they start from the
same cross.

5. Measure how far
the car goes.

Who pushed the
car the farthest?

Who used the
most force?

Glossary and Further Information

brake a device for making a bicycle, car, or other vehicle slow down or stop

direction the place that something is heading toward

electricity a form of energy that is used to work some machines

force something that makes a thing move, or changes the way it is moving

machine a device made by people to do a particular thing

natural something that is made by nature

pedal the part of a machine that you push with your foot to make something move

vehicle a machine that carries people and things from one place to another

Books

Give it a Push! Give it a Pull!: A Look at Forces
by Jennifer Boothroyd
(Lerner Publications, 2010)

Push and Pull
by Charlotte Guillain
(Heinemann-Raintree, 2008)

Why it Works: Pushes and Pulls
by Anna Claybourne
(QED Publishing, 2008)

Index